RAINBOW VISION JOURNAL

RED

How to follow your heart
and find your bliss
without reliving your past

SHARON DAWN

Published by: Rainbow Vision Journal
                 PO Box 1062, Airlie Beach, Qld, Australia 4802
                 www.rainbowvisionjournal.com
                 Email: smile@rainbowvisionjournal.com

Cover Design by: Meltproject
Illustrations by: Sharon Dawn
Typeset by: Adam Press

ISBN Hardcover: 978-0-6487662-0-9
ISBN Paperback: 978-0-6487662-2-3
ISBN eBook: 978-0-6487662-1-6

 A catalogue record for this work is available from the National Library of Australia

Copyright © 2020. All rights reserved. No part of this publication may be reproduced in any manner without prior written permission from the publisher.

The information given in this journal should not be used as a substitute for professional medical advice. Any use of the information in this journal is at the reader's discretion and risk. Readers who are experiencing adverse effects from any situation arising from using this journal should seek professional counselling. Neither the author nor the publisher can be held responsible for any loss, claim or damage arising from use, or misuse, of the suggestions made in this journal.

DEDICATION

I dedicate this journal to women who desire a change.

CONTENTS

WHAT IS RAINBOW VISION JOURNAL — vii

FREE GIFTS — ix

HOW TO USE THIS JOURNAL — 1

    I am Silent and Listen — 7
    Catching My Chaser Thoughts — 9
    Finding My Gold Nuggets — 11
    I am so Grateful for — 13

WHAT I LOVE — 15

    My Favourite Things — 17
    My 5 Most Enjoyable Things to Do — 19
    I Feel Happy When… — 21
    My Favourite Songs — 23
    My Most Favourite Memories — 25
    What I Loved as a Child — 27
    What I Loved as a Teen — 29
    Add more Love into my Life — 31
    What I Love about ME — 35
    I AM — 37
    How I Feel Today — 39
    RED Daily Ritual — 41
    My Number One Relationship — 43
    Who I Love Most — 45
    Journal Time – Love — 46

HOW IS MY SUPPORT — 57

Where do I get Support? — 59
My Heart — 61
My Friends — 63
Who do I take for Granted? — 65
Who Inspires Me? — 67
Local Community Support — 69
Online Community Support — 71
My Environment — 73
What Grounds Me? — 75
Add more Support to my Life — 77
Grounding Exercise — 79
Journal Time – Support — 80

LET'S GET CREATIVE — 87

RED Words — 88
RED Thoughts — 89
Create a Loving Board — 91
Wall of Hearts — 93
Fill my Jar with Love — 95
Scribble Time — 96

BRING IT ALL TOGETHER — 101

It's Magic — 103
Revising my Chaser Thoughts — 107
The Magic Rewritten — 111
3 Action Steps — 117
My Reward — 119
Congratulations! — 121
What's Next? — 123
Journal Time – Keep up the Magic — 124

RED — My Heart

How to follow your heart and find your bliss without reliving your past.

ORANGE — My Experiences

How to have awesome experiences without worrying about time or money.

YELLOW — My Well-being

How to feel good regardless of your body shape or fitness level.

GREEN — My Abundance

How to attract money and abundance into your life without the stress.

BLUE — My Purpose

How to discover your true purpose regardless of your location and skill.

INDIGO — My Awareness

How to stay in control of your thoughts regardless of your situation.

VIOLET — My Connection

How to feel connected and thankful regardless of your faith or religion.

 GOLD — My Uniqueness

How to bring your life into alignment using your Rainbow Vision Steps.

What is the RAINBOW VISION JOURNAL?

The Rainbow Vision Journal is a series of eight workbook journals that take you on a journey to discover your true self and your inner purpose.

Rainbow

Signifies new beginnings as you break through your current path, just as the sun breaks through the clouds after rain. The bridge symbolises your journey, leading you to your pot of gold.

Rainbows are a magical light that make us feel peaceful. They raise our energy vibration while reminding us that life is not always as we see it.

Vision

You have the ability to imagine, to create images and to plan your future. With vision you can look within, to see your true wisdom.

Journal

A safe place where you can capture your thoughts and ideas, plan your future and release your past. A place where you can be honest with yourself. A place where you can be creative.

ACKNOWLEDGEMENTS

I would like to thank my husband who loves me for who I am and supports me in every adventurous path I choose to follow.

I would also like to thank all the creative and inspirational people in the world. You continue to inspire me and enhance my journey.

A special thank you to The Regional Arts Development Fund (RADF) for supporting the publishing of this journal. It is a privilege to receive your support.

The Regional Arts Development Fund is a Queensland Government and Whitsunday Regional Council Partnership to support local arts and culture in regional Queensland.

FREE GIFTS

As a thank you for purchasing this journal please accept the following gifts. They will assist you on your journey by giving extra support and motivation.

- Download a guided meditation to do prior to journaling. This is a quick meditation that takes you into your heart.

  Go to *www.sharondawn.com.au/meditation*

- Receive the monthly Rainbow Vision Journal eNewsletter for support and clarity on the topics discussed in this journal. All promotions and specials will be released via the eNewsletter prior to release on the website and Social Media. To Register, go to *www.rainbowvisionjournal.com* and click on 'Subscribe to eNewsletter.'

- Download the Rainbow Vision Journal support eBook for free.

  This eBook explains the ideas behind Rainbow Vision Journal including your inner child, energy vibration and the law of attraction. It discusses how the key to a great life is to be aware of our thoughts and feelings so we can align them to our heart's desire.

  www.rainbowvisionjournal.com

- Join a PRIVATE Facebook group specifically to support anyone completing this journal. Email *smile@rainbowvisionjournal.com* for your on-going support.

- Follow me on Facebook and Instagram and become part of the ongoing journey of awareness and inner connection.

  Sharon Dawn and Rainbow Vision Journal

  @rainbow_vision_journal

- The GOLD journal will be made available for free to all readers who purchase the other seven. Conditions apply so keep your receipts.

*You can follow your heart and find your bliss
when you make a conscious decision to forget the past*

x

How to Use This Journal

To follow our heart and find our bliss, we must first open our heart and our mind. When we have suffered from abuse, hardship, bullying or depression, we shut down, we go within, we hide, and often that's where we stay. We wonder why we feel like something is wrong or missing in our life. We wonder why life is not quite like we imagined it would be. We wonder why we feel frustrated or even angry sometimes. On the surface we have learnt to accept the way our life is and hide our feelings, yet we have a deeper knowing that we could have more. We feel an inner yearning to be someone other than who we are, yet we usually ignore it.

Journaling connects us to our inner self. It lets us explore what we have buried deep inside. It allows us to say things that we might not tell others, to talk about our innermost thoughts and feelings in a safe place. It allows us to come out of hiding and embrace the person we are meant to be.

Before you start journaling, set an intention for yourself. Choose something that makes you feel strong and excited.

E.g. I am so excited that today I am exploring my true heart's desire.

Then, take a few minutes to go within and connect to your heart.

As you start to connect, let the answers come to you as you let your inner child guide you. Don't force any answer, instead allow it to come through. Usually the first answer you receive is the most accurate for you. If you are unsure, the easy way to tell is if it feels kind and loving, it comes from your heart, and if it feels harsh, judgmental or criticising in any way, it is your chaser thought (your sub-conscious programming).

You can download my free meditation at
www.sharondawn.com.au/meditation

When you connect to your heart in this way, you will receive guidance from within. It may be a quick flash thought or image in your head and it will feel right for you. You can call this guidance whatever you like; God, Goddess, soul, angels, intuition; or you can think of this as your inner child talking to you. From here on, it will be referred to as your inner child and you can put your own name to it if you choose. As you write or draw in this journal, you are encouraged to allow your inner child to guide you. It takes practice to hear these messages but when you do, it opens up a whole new level of support, one you can truly rely on.

The left-hand pages in this journal are for you to capture any ideas that can help clarify your inner self. Paste in pictures of anything you like, use colours, patterns and doodles. Add whatever makes you smile and allows you to play. Let your imagination go wild, add crazy images and ideas. Decide to get out of your own way and just have fun.

This first section is designed for you to use throughout the RED journal. You will go back to it many times as you become aware of new things about yourself. The first page is 'I am Silent and Listen.' It is to encourage you to set aside times to be silent and let your inner child come through. We all have at least one-minute spare here and there throughout our day so make the commitment to start listening from within.

Next is a page called 'Catching My Chaser Thoughts,' This is where you write any thoughts that are disempowering to you. These thoughts usually come after a positive thought. E.g. (Thought) I would love to sing, (Chaser) I can't sing, who am I to sing? Capture as many of these as you can, and you will work on them later in this journal. Write what pops into your head. Do not analyse it, write it exactly how it comes to you.

When I think good thoughts, I feel good

Next is 'Finding My Gold Nuggets.' On this page, capture any 'aha' moments. Anything that seems perfect to you. These become part of your pot of gold at the end of the rainbow, part of your bliss. The last page in this section is called 'I am so Grateful for.' This page reminds you of the wonderful things that happen each day. The warm bed you slept in, the food in your tummy, the clothes on your back, the butterfly that fluttered past, the smile from a stranger. Life becomes so busy and so automatic that we forget to stop and be thankful. Every day try and think of at least five different things to be grateful for. It is a great way to start your day.

When I stop to be thankful, I see so much more to be thankful for

To get the most out of this journal, aim to complete only one or two pages at a time. Don't rush it. Think deeply about each question and see what comes to you, then journal further on your thoughts. Each page is designed to open your awareness as to what is buried deep within. Let your feelings guide you. If it feels good, it is right for you. If it makes you feel uncomfortable, it may be because you are avoiding something, so ask yourself if you want to explore that thought further or let it go. If a thought makes you feel bad, or it lowers your energy vibration and makes you feel heavy, then beware. That is your warning sign that it is probably not for you.

As you work through the RED journal, try to avoid criticising yourself for past events or wishing it all away. Everything in your life is part of your journey. Those experiences are unique to you and they make you who you are. Sure, you have experiences that were not good, but by accepting both the good and the bad of who you are, you move forward in creating the life you deserve, the life you are meant to have.

This journal is for finding what you really love and what makes you happy. It is for raising your energy vibration to be the best you. It is not designed for you to look back into your past and dig it up. We all have a story and when we continue to tell it, we stay in that story, in that low energy vibration. When we choose to let go of our story and look forward, we raise our vibration. We start forming new habits with our new thoughts, enhancing who we choose to be.

When we let go of the past, we can redefine our future

Sometimes, however, our past is still very much on our mind and we struggle to let it go. If this is you, then whenever you feel your past taking over, grab a piece of paper and write it all out. Write everything that is on your mind, whatever you are upset or stressed about. It is usually the same broken record that keeps playing and it's time to release it. That broken record is part of the past and no matter how often you replay it, you can't change it. Once you realise the broken record is affecting your present moment because you are reliving it in the now, then you can see it is time to release it. So, write it all out. All the hurt, all the events that are clinging to you. Once you have finished writing, fold it in half, then half again. Put it in a bowl, light a match and burn it. Say to yourself 'I now release my past.' As it burns, imagine all that stress, anxiety and past rubbish is being released. Let it flow out of you. You may choose to make it a celebrational ceremony as you let it all go.

Life gives us hurts and sad times, just as it gives us happy times; however, as you become aware of your thoughts and feelings, you begin to see that it is your response that defines your outcomes. How you respond to any given incident is a choice you make, either consciously or unconsciously. You are responding to things all day, every day. When you become aware of this, you learn to make these decisions consciously. You learn to choose what is important to you, and you see how your choices can stop your suffering. You then find peace in accepting what is out of your control.

It is the same for your inner thoughts. The more you become aware of these thoughts and how they control you, the more you will find ways in which you can change your thinking and therefore your reaction to something. Simply by being aware and making a conscious choice of how you want to react, allows you to become the person you wish to be. We all have the ability to choose our thoughts and reactions once we learn to be aware of what is really happening in our head. What we choose, determines how our life unfolds.

Think of this journal as an adventure into your heart. It is a way for you to discover your true self and to release your inner child, and free yourself from restraints, rules and judgments. Give yourself permission to explore, play, imagine and draw like a child. When you are stuck, ask yourself 'why' just as a child does. Let things like judgement and resentment start to drop away. Focus on creating a happy place where you can come back regularly to remind yourself of what is in your heart.

Keep asking

'Am I following my heart? Am I being true to myself?'

THOUGHTS

Write or draw your thoughts

I am Silent and Listen

When you stop and let your mind be still, even for a moment, you open a space that allows your inner child's voice to be heard.

To quieten your mind and bring it to stillness, simply take 3 deep breaths in and out. Focus on your breath and let your mind fall into a space that has no thoughts. When a thought floats in, observe it, then let it go as you bring your focus back to the breath.

FIND MOMENTS TO BE PRESENT

I can be silent and in the moment when I brush my teeth, have a shower, make the bed, or even as I am waiting for the jug to boil.

Download your free meditation www.sharondawn.com.au/meditation

THOUGHTS

Write or draw your thoughts

Catching My Chaser Thoughts

As you work through each exercise, negative thoughts may pop into your head. What are you saying to yourself when you are not paying attention? Write whatever come into your mind.

Do not analyse or change it, simply capture it here.

E.g. I can't do this, no one supports me, what a waste of time.

....
....
....
....
....
....
....
....
....
....
....
....

*When you are aware of your self-talk,
you can change what does not serve you*

THOUGHTS
Write or draw your thoughts

Finding My Gold Nuggets

Capture any inspiring thoughts, words, sayings, memories or 'aha' moments that motivate or inspire you.

This makes up part of your pot of gold at the end of the rainbow.

-
-
-
-
-
-
-
-
-
-
-
-
-
-
-
-

I consciously choose to live in love every day for the rest of my life

THOUGHTS

Write or draw your thoughts

I am so Grateful for

Giving thanks for the love and support in your life raises your energy vibration. Being grateful reminds you of the wonderful things you have in your life. It allows you to appreciate them in this moment as well as attract those loving energies back to you again.

WE ATTRACT WHAT WE FOCUS ON

_____

_____

_____

_____

_____

_____

_____

_____

_____

_____

_____

_____

_____

Thank You, Thank You, Thank You

Love and awareness create empowerment and freedom

WHAT I LOVE

We all need love. This section is to remind you of what you love most so you can include these things into your daily life. They also help you when you feel sad and need a pick-me-up. Think about what puts a smile on your face, and what makes you feel full of love. The more love you feel each day, the higher your energy vibration and the happier you are.

The three sections, LOVE, SUPPORT and CREATE can be completed in any order that feels right for you.

There are two pages in the LOVE section, 'What I Loved as a Child' and 'What I Loved as a Teen,' that may bring up unpleasant memories. If so, skip them or write out the memories and burn them. These pages are here to remind you of your childhood loves, to see if you can bring some of that magic back into your life. They are not here to dredge up past hurts.

Happiness is something inside us, it is not a destination.

The suggested daily ritual is to help you expand your energy vibration and feel the love you have within. You can do this at any time during the day; however, if you start your morning with this ritual and the intention to feel loving, you are setting yourself up to have a great day.

At the end of each section is 'Journal Time' where you are encouraged to explore the thoughts further. Write or draw using your imagination to focus on what you love and what else makes you happy.

THOUGHTS

Write or draw your thoughts

My Favourite Things

Sometimes we need to remind ourselves of what we love most in life, and why. It's time to remember all those wonderful things so you can put more into your daily life.

My favourite…	What it is	How it makes me feel
Colour		
Food/Drink		
Type of music		
Song		
Movie		
TV series		
Fairy-tale		
Book		
Self-pamper		
Activity		
Place to walk		
Location to visit		
Flower		
Tree		
Animal		
Bird		
Insect		
Time of year		
Time of day		
Jewellery		
Outfit		

THOUGHTS
Write or draw your thoughts

My 5 Most Enjoyable Things to Do

1) ....

Why? ....

....

2) ....

Why? ....

....

3) ....

Why? ....

....

4) ....

Why? ....

....

5) ....

Why? ....

....

THOUGHTS

Write or draw your thoughts

I Feel Happy When…

Now that you have your list of favourite things, let's include what else you really love. What do you enjoy seeing, hearing or doing most?

I love to smell flowers, listen to wind chimes, walk barefoot in sand.

These reminders come in handy when you want to de-stress your day.

♥ ....
....

♥ ....
....

♥ ....
....

♥ ....
....

♥ ....
....

My day is full of things I LOVE

THOUGHTS
Write or draw your thoughts

My Favourite Songs

We all react to music. The energy vibration of the notes touches our energy vibration. Songs can make us laugh or cry.

Create two lists of songs you love. One for relaxing and the second to sing out loud, dance and really feel energised. Use daily.

Relaxed	Energised

THOUGHTS

Write or draw your thoughts

My Most Favourite Memories

Happy memories have the power to transform how we feel in any given moment. When we feel down, we can find it hard to pull ourselves up again; however, if you have a fantastic memory and you put yourself into that memory, you will feel your energy vibration start to rise. As soon as you do, put a smile on your face and you will feel even better.

THE ONLY TIME WE SHOULD LOOK BACK IS TO ENJOY A HAPPY MEMORY

Capture the top 3 memories you have that no matter what, make you feel AWESOME!

1) ....
   ....
   ....

2) ....
   ....
   ....

3) ....
   ....
   ....

My golden memories

THOUGHTS

Write or draw your thoughts

What I Loved as a Child

When we are young, we do what naturally makes us happy.

We had restrictions in our environment but not on our imagination.

What were your favourite stories, games and activities?

What did you want to be when you grew up?

♥ ....
....

♥ ....
....

♥ ....
....

♥ ....
....

♥ ....
....

Are you doing any of these things now? Could you?

THOUGHTS

Write or draw your thoughts

What I Loved as a Teen

When we are teenagers, we look at things differently. It is a time when we are trying to find who we are and therefore we push boundaries.

What did you love and what got you inspired? What did you do for fun?

♥ ....
....

♥ ....
....

♥ ....
....

♥ ....
....

♥ ....
....

♥ ....
....

Would you like to bring any of these back into your life?

THOUGHTS
Write or draw your thoughts

Add more Love into my Life

The more love you feel for yourself and within yourself, the more love you have to give others.

Here are some suggestions. List below what works for you.

- ♥ Make a habit to show myself love and appreciation every day.
- ♥ Create ME time. Schedule times when I do things just for myself.
- ♥ Do something special for those I am close to.
- ♥ Spend time around animals.
- ♥ Appreciate the incredible harmony of nature. Listen to birds, watch ants, sit on the grass, soak up a sunset, face the sun and just breathe.

What I Love about ME

We can be quick to criticise our looks or our behaviour, yet we forget to celebrate all the wonderful things we have to offer, like how amazing our smile is, or how our mind helps us solve problems, or even how our body carries us throughout our life.

Remember to catch any chaser thoughts you feel about yourself.

I LOVE

♥ ....
♥ ....
♥ ....
♥ ....
♥ ....
♥ ....
♥ ....
♥ ....
♥ ....
♥ ....
♥ ....
♥ ....

Circle the 3 things you love most about yourself.

I AM

In the left column write all the labels you identify with
Eg Mother, Wife, Artist, Writer, Gardener, Traveller

In the right column write everything positive about yourself
Eg Smart, Loving, Happy, Kind, Relaxed, Friendly

Include anything you wish you were but don't think you are
Eg Relaxed, Fit, Happy

HAPPINESS STARTS WHEN WE ACCEPT OURSELVES FOR WHO WE ARE

I am a	I AM ....
I am a	I AM ....
I am a	I AM ....
I am a	I AM ....
I am a	I AM ....
I am a	I AM ....
I am a	I AM ....
I am a	I AM ....

Look over your list. Do you have any resistant or negative thoughts?
If so, write these thoughts on your chaser page.

Circle 3 statements on each side that make you feel strong and energised.

1 2 3 4 5 6 7 8 9 10
_____ __ / __ / __

1 2 3 4 5 6 7 8 9 10
_____ __ / __ / __

1 2 3 4 5 6 7 8 9 10
_____ __ / __ / __

1 2 3 4 5 6 7 8 9 10
_____ __ / __ / __

1 2 3 4 5 6 7 8 9 10
_____ __ / __ / __

1 2 3 4 5 6 7 8 9 10
_____ __ / __ / __

1 2 3 4 5 6 7 8 9 10
_____ __ / __ / __

1 2 3 4 5 6 7 8 9 10
_____ __ / __ / __

1 2 3 4 5 6 7 8 9 10
_____ __ / __ / __

How I Feel Today

It is easy to feel sad or sorry for ourselves. It is easy to feel mad or frustrated. These feelings are routine for us until we become truly aware of how often they float around in our mind yet do not help us. They feel comforting, yet it is a false sense of comfort, because they don't actually make us feel better. We all have the power to feel great, we just need to relearn how to do it.

Think of your feelings as a ladder. If you are at the bottom rung then it is a challenge to immediately step onto the top rung. Our feelings are similar. When we feel grief, we then climb up to anger, then courage, acceptance, reason and love. Make a commitment to yourself to monitor how you feel each day with the intention to feel better today than you did yesterday. Keep track of where you are by circling the number and putting in the date. Write down whatever happened to lift you up or pull you down the ladder. Could you have chosen a different reaction?

1   2   3   4   5   6   7   8   9   10

_____   __ / __ / __

1   2   3   4   5   6   7   8   9   10

_____   __ / __ / __

1   2   3   4   5   6   7   8   9   10

_____   __ / __ / __

1   2   3   4   5   6   7   8   9   10

_____   __ / __ / __

Every day I aim for one step higher

Loving myself is the greatest thing I can learn

RED Daily Ritual

When you start your morning with an intention, it determines how you want your day to be.

Although this exercise is good at the start of the day, you can do it anywhere at any time.

- ♥ Get comfortable and take a deep breath in and hold it, then let all your breath out and hold. Do three deep breaths then breathe normally.
- ♥ Focus on your breathing, as it flows evenly in and out. This allows you to be completely in the moment.
- ♥ Feel how relaxed your body becomes. Observe without thinking. If one part is tense, bring your attention to it, then breath in relaxation to it and let the tension go.
- ♥ Place a smile onto your face and relax some more.
- ♥ Keep breathing at a normal rate, focusing on your breath.
- ♥ Place your hand over your heart, gently rub in a circular motion.
- ♥ Now repeat this little mantra as you breathe in and out.

I LOVE, I LOVE, I LOVE, I LOVE

- ♥ Let the energy of that mantra flow throughout your body.

During the day if you feel stressed or overwhelmed, simply focus on your breath, put your hand on your heart, and say the mantra

My Number One Relationship

When we have been in any relationship with a friend, family member or lover for a long time, we are inclined to form habits on how we communicate and treat each other. We may be taking them for granted yet expecting attention in return.

Who is the number one person in my life?
....

What do I love most about them?
....

What do I think they love most about me?
....
....

What is one special thing I could do to make them happy?
....
....

How can I tell them what that is?
....
....

What is something I can do every day to show I love them?
....

Who I Love Most

Think about that number one person in your life, what do you really want to say to them? Imagine they are standing in front of you, smiling, listening and not answering.

What would you like to say?

Write out a loving, honest talk you could have with them, telling them how you truly feel.

Journal Time – Love

When I feel supported, I know I can achieve anything

How is my support

As women, we often give support to our families, yet we are not always so good at asking for, or accepting, support in return. When you give and receive support, you feel valued and worthy, which then increases your confidence and self-esteem.

When I give, I receive

In this section, look to where you can increase your support. It may be in the form of finding a new hobby or community interest where you can use your knowledge and skill to help others. There are many great causes that you can belong to, and the best way to start is by knowing what you love, and then knowing what areas in your life need topping up with support and friendships.

A mind map is a great tool to dig deeper into your thoughts. You can use this whenever you are trying to work out what you want yet feel a little stuck. It is an excellent planning tool, that helps you clear your mind and it is a fun way to expand your ideas.

I love and honour myself by connecting to my support network

Journal at the end of this section to see how you can improve the support you give and receive. Remember It's OK to remove people from your life that do not make you feel good. Family and friends are important, but not everyone deserves to be a part of your life.

You should not feel guilty when you choose to do something for yourself

MINDMAP

Where do I get Support?

Knowing who inspires you and who drains you, can help you determine where to spend your time and where you should put strategies in place to protect yourself. It is also important to know where you can get support when you feel down, need help or just need a hug.

Who supports me at home? ....

At work? ....

Which family members and friends really support me?

....

....

How else do I feel supported? ....

....

....

Do I feel I have enough support in my life? .... Yes / No

If No, how can I find more support for myself? ....

....

If I was stuck on a deserted island for a month, who would I want with me?

....

Why would I choose this person? ....

....

THOUGHTS

Write or draw your thoughts

My Heart

Think about all the people in your life and place everyone that makes you feel great into your heart. Leave out anyone that does not make you feel good. It's OK to remove yourself from anyone who does not make you feel good, even if they are family.

These are the people who empower me

THOUGHTS
Write or draw your thoughts

My Friends

Your friends are who comfort and support you, they also energise and inspire you. Family members may be your friends too, but not always. Often we have different relationships with different friends. It is great to know who to turn to for a hug, for a conversation or for inspiration. List below your close friends and think about how each one supports you and how you support them.

1) .... gives me ....
....
....

I give them ....
....
....

2) .... gives me ....
....
....

I give them ....
....
....

3) .... gives me ....
....
....

I give them ....
....

THOUGHTS

Write or draw your thoughts

Who do I take for Granted?

Unfortunately, as humans, we sometimes take our friends or family for granted, especially those who mean the most to us.

Who do I take for granted?

....
....
....
....

What can I do to show more appreciation?

....
....
....
....
....
....
....
....
....
....

THOUGHTS

Write or draw your thoughts

Who Inspires Me?

People who inspire you, can also teach you many things. When you watch and read how they talk, act and treat others, you get a real sense of who that person is. When you have role models, you can learn to be the person you want to be.

Sometimes there are some real gems of people right under your nose.

10 people who inspire me and why:

1. .... Why: ....
2. .... Why: ....
3. .... Why: ....
4. .... Why: ....
5. .... Why: ....
6. .... Why: ....
7. .... Why: ....
8. .... Why: ....
9. .... Why: ....
10. .... Why: ....

What do they have in common?

....

....

How can I make that part of my life?

....

....

MIND MAP TO FIND WHAT I WOULD LOVE TO SUPPORT

Think about what you love most. This could be anything from being with people, working with animals, or doing creative activities. Then think about what that could lead to, and what is available in your community. Think outside the square.

E.g. Say you love horses, and you realise that you just love being around them, that it's not important if you ride them. Then think about how much time you would like to commit, if you could go and play with horses. Next look at what is available in your community. You might decide riding for the disabled appeals to you as it covers everything you love.

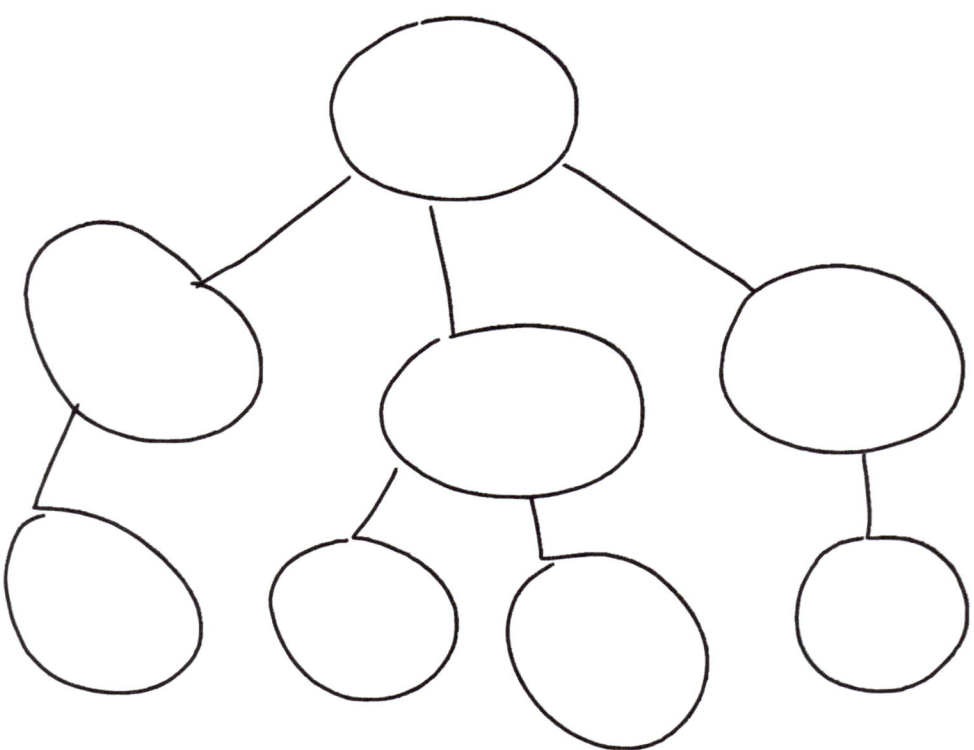

I feel supported when I am involved with like-minded people

Local Community Support

It is very fulfilling helping others in your community. By being involved, you may find you get more out of the experience than you expect. You get to meet new people and have new experiences. If you don't already support a community group, think of an area that may excite you. Use the mind map to gain clarity.

What groups do I belong to in my area?

How do they support me?

How do I support them?

How do they energise me? (If they don't energise, how can you get out of it?)

Is there something else I could join that would inspire me? (Use the mind map on the opposite page)

Online Community Support

We are so lucky to live in an era where we can easily connect with like-minded people from all around the world. Social media has become a big part of our daily life and when you are smart about it, you can ignore all the negative groups, and simply belong to private groups that support and empower.

What groups do I belong to online?

1) .... 2) ....
3) .... 4) ....

How do they support me?

1) .... 2) ....
3) .... 4) ....

How do I support them?

1) .... 2) ....
3) .... 4) ....

Could I get more out of these groups?
....

Do I support them because I want to, or feel I must?
....
....

Is there something else I could join that would inspire me?
....
....

Join the Rainbow Vision Journal Private Support.

THOUGHTS

Write or draw your thoughts

My Environment

Have a look to see how your environment supports you.

Where is my favourite spot to chill out?

....

....

Do I go here often?   Yes / No   Could I?   Yes / No

How do I relax when I feel stressed? *(Meditate, take a bath, walk)*

....

....

How do I connect to nature? *(Garden, walk barefoot, watch birds?)*

....

....

Could I be in nature more often?

....

....

What animals are in my life?

....

....

How do they make me feel?

....

....

THOUGHTS
Write or draw your thoughts

What Grounds Me?

There are many ways to feel grounded. You can meditate or be still.
Do creative activities like drawing, painting, writing, music.
Go for walks, sit in nature, use crystals, play with animals or play music.
Spending time with your loved ones can also be grounding.

How do I feel grounded?

What could I add into my life to feel more grounded?

I feel grounded by the love I have for myself, my family and friends

Add more Support to my Life

Have a think about where else you can add support into your life.

Here are some suggestions. List below what works for you.

- ♥ Stay in regular contact with specific friends and family who make me feel good.
- ♥ Listen more intently when people are talking to me.
- ♥ Be aware when someone needs help and ask what I can do for them.
- ♥ Congratulate people when they do something they are proud of.
- ♥ Reach out and say hello to strangers.
- ♥ Create a habit of smiling and talking nicely to everyone I meet.

....

....

....

....

....

....

....

....

When we appreciate others, we are also appreciated more

Grounding Exercise

**Sometimes we need to stop and take time to reconnect within.
Try this little exercise.**

- ♥ Walk in nature, go barefoot on the grass, sand or dirt.
- ♥ Stop, be still and breathe deeply.
- ♥ Visualise connecting with the earth energy. Imagine it coming up from the core of the earth, into your feet, up your legs and into your heart then expanding out.
- ♥ Feel it nurturing you and flowing throughout your body.
- ♥ Think about who you love, who inspires and energises you.
- ♥ Feel their love and support in your heart.
- ♥ Feel thankful for what you have in your life.
- ♥ Reflect on how relaxed and grounded you feel now.
- ♥ Smile and feel the loving energy vibrate throughout your body.
- ♥ Give yourself permission to be happy

Be still and feel love

Journal Time – Support

We are all Creative, we just need to believe that is true.

LET'S GET CREATIVE

This section is designed to bring together your most cherished thoughts, ideas, people and objects. It is up to you what you include. The intention is to make something that reminds you to feel good every day. To create something that helps you keep your energy vibration high.

When we create, we let go of our internal chatter

Writing, craft, art and music are some of the things that help you connect within, which is why journaling is so good for you. Look over everything you have already decided works for you then take your favourite thoughts and bring them together to have some creative fun.

On the next couple of pages, you will also find some words and empowering statements. These are prompts only. Use whatever inspires you to create your unique reminders.

Often when we try something new we expect perfection. Don't let perfection get in the way of doing something. Even the greatest painters, writers and musicians all started from scratch. They practiced and committed long hours to achieve the results they did. You, on the other hand, can simply let your inner child come out and play. Let go of the idea that you can't do it, and allow yourself to just try, you may be pleasantly surprised at how much fun you have. Let the child in you be creative, then, when someone says, 'that looks like a child did it,' you will know you have successfully achieved your goal!

Children think everything they create is a masterpiece, because it is

Please remember, do not judge, simply be kind to yourself and enjoy the process. Creating releases stress and clears our thinking. It raises our energy vibration and allows us to be free.

RED Words

Circle the words that you feel the most connected to. You may want to use some of these when you create your inspiration board.

Love	Relationships	Passion	Romance
Hugs	Emotion	Compassion	Heart
Intensity	Desire	Life	Sexy
Brilliance	Vitality	Charm	Survival
Excitement	Energy	Courage	Strength
Home	Warmth	Support	Safe
Determination	Empowerment	Encouragement	Stimulation
Comforting	Attention	Sensuality	Arouse
Family	Partner	Children	Pets
Friends	Nurture	Success	Birds
Networks	Connections	Social	Nature
Independence	Devotion	Unity	Plants
Culture	Grounded	Base Chakra	Animals
Awareness	Thrill	Sunrise	Fire
Flowers	Sunset	Gemstone	Rocks

RED Thoughts

Find or create a statement that makes you feel AWESOME.

I love and honour myself	I am strong
I create freedom with love and awareness	I love myself
I live a life of love and gratitude	I am worthy
I joyfully help others	I am free to be me
What can I do for the people I love?	Its cool to be me
I accept who I am now as I learn to evolve into my true self	I attract love into my life
When I think good thoughts, I feel good	I am safe
I attract what I think about	My life is magical
I surround myself with people who raise my vibration	I choose to be me
I have decided to become the person I want to be	I get what I focus on
All change begins with a brave decision	I am vibrational energy
Love and happiness are already within me	I deserve me time
I treat myself how I expect others to treat me	I am grateful
I am true to myself	I trust myself
I have unconditional love for myself	I can create
I get what I give	I follow my heart

THOUGHTS

Write or draw your thoughts

Create a Loving Board

This creative exercise gives you a visual reminder of the things you love. You can make a board about your friends or family, or a board with all the things you like.

- ♥ Set the intention of what you would like your board to represent.
- ♥ Select a nice photo of yourself so you can be surrounded with love.
- ♥ Gather photos or images of things you wish to include. Use old magazines for extra images.
- ♥ Select a nice board or canvas, A3 card is great.
- ♥ Paint a background on your board or keep it white.
- ♥ Write out, print or cut from magazines any affirmations and words that make you feel good.
- ♥ Scatter your pictures around the board to see what layout feels good.
- ♥ For inspiration, read through your journal answers before you start.
- ♥ Let your imagination create the collage. There is no right or wrong way. Simply enjoy creating your vision.
- ♥ Most important - HAVE FUN.

SAMPLE IDEAS

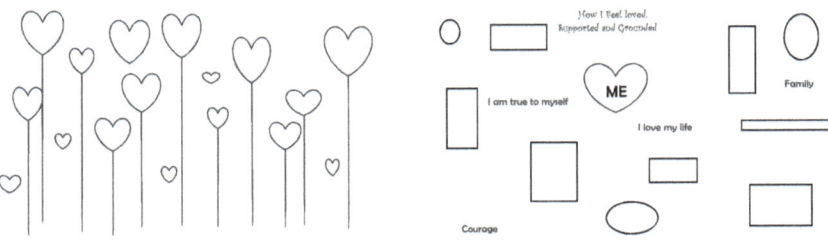

Place your board where you can see it, so it becomes a constant reminder for you.

THOUGHTS

Write or draw your thoughts

Wall of Hearts

Create hearts with affirmations or other inspiring words or images that make you feel good. You can do as many hearts as you want and put them all on a board or keep them as individual ones. You could do different shapes or simply do a wall of inspiring thoughts.

Place the finished project, on the fridge or wall, or have a screen saver on your computer.

Place it so you see it each day as a reminder of what inspires you.

Experiment with pictures of things you like and add words that inspire you

THOUGHTS

Write or draw your thoughts

Fill my Jar with Love

Create a jar and add lots of lovely little sayings into it. Write something in each box below, then cut up the boxes, fold each in half and place it into your jar.

You may prefer to get a separate piece of paper

Be creative with uplifting and fun affirmations or images of what you enjoy. When you need a little pick-me-up, choose one from the jar.

SCRIBBLE

Draw and let your pen do what it wants

SCRIBBLE

Draw and let your pen do what it wants

SCRIBBLE
Draw and let your pen do what it wants

SCRIBBLE

Draw and let your pen do what it wants

*We are so lucky, sometimes we need to
remind ourselves how blessed we really are*

BRING IT ALL TOGETHER

In this section you are encouraged to be imaginative like a child. To let your child come out and play and explore those things that excite you. Think about your favourite fairy tale, what is it that really captures you? Is it the romance? Is it the adventure or the happy ever after? Maybe it is the possibility of a totally different world to live in, a world of make-believe. Whatever it is, use that excitement to write your imaginary magic life. Then you will revise your chaser thoughts and rewrite your magic story in a way that inspires you even more.

Whatever you write in your magic story make it feel exciting, like a magical dream come true. Once you have revised your story, you will set up three action steps to bring some of that magic into your life now. To keep you on your path, you will also establish a reward that inspires you to stay on your path.

E.g. you might want to learn to paint, because it is relaxing, and you feel great afterwards. So, find an artist or a YouTube channel to teach you, then commit to 15 minutes a day. As a reward, buy yourself a quality brush or frame one picture a month.

You are encouraged to continue journaling every day, even if it is just one or two pages where you write, draw, scribble or doodle. In 'The Artists Way', author Julia Cameron recommends writing 3 pages a day as a release to reach your creativity. Writing gives clarity by opening your mind to new perspectives and possibilities. It releases stress and anxiety to fill you with happiness and self-worth. Every day do something creative for yourself and something that makes you feel special so you can keep your energy vibration high and enjoy the pleasures available to you. You are not too busy to dedicate 15 minutes a day to you, especially since that 15 minutes will make you feel good, help you de-stress and help you relax.

Life is to be enjoyed, so do what you love

THOUGHTS

Write or draw your thoughts

It's Magic

You have a magical wand and you have three wishes to expand the love in your life. Take your three wishes and create a fairy-tale story, an imaginary story about how you would love to live. You can be anyone, do anything, live anywhere, in any time, in this world or another. It can be fantasy or real.

If you close your eyes, where would you really love to be? What do you look like? What does it feel like? Who would be with you? What are you doing? Describe how it FEELS.

Before writing, take time to be still and go within. Feel yourself full of love before you ask your inner child to help select three wishes and then ask for help to write your fairy-tale.

WISHES

1) ....
2) ....
3) ....

Life is magical when I live in the high energy vibrations of love and gratitude

Revising my Chaser Thoughts

Go back to your chaser page and have a good look at what you have captured. These negative thoughts come from your belief system and outside influences from when you were very young. None of them are true, although they seem true when you hear them.

A thought from your heart, from your inner self, is always loving and supportive, NEVER negative. A thought from your mind is usually judgmental, criticising or disempowering in some way. It is simply how the sub-conscious mind gets programmed.

To understand this better, download the *Rainbow Vision Journal* free eBook.

Look at each chaser thought and see if there are any recurring patterns or themes. Then take each thought and create an empowering statement from it. E.g. I'm no good at this stuff can become, I am good at what I choose to do, or, I'm hopeless can become, I trust in myself.

Old thought ....
....
New empowering thought ....
....
Old thought ....
....
New empowering thought ....
....
Old thought ....
....
New empowering thought ....
....

Old thought ....
....

New empowering thought ....
....

Old thought ....
....

New empowering thought ....
....

Old thought ....
....

New empowering thought ....
....

Old thought ....
....

New empowering thought ....
....

Old thought ....
....

New empowering thought ....
....

Old thought ....
....

New empowering thought ....
....

Old thought ....
....

New empowering thought ....
....

Old thought ....
....

New empowering thought ....
....

Old thought ....
....

New empowering thought ....
....

Old thought ....
....

New empowering thought ....
....

THOUGHTS
Write or draw your thoughts

The Magic Rewritten

Now that you know your magical story and you also know the self-talk that has been holding you back, it's time to rewrite the magic.

Ask yourself, what similarities are there between your real and magical worlds? Match up people, places and things from your magical world into your real world. Ask yourself what fits together, what feels right and what is missing. Is it uplifting? Does it make you want to embrace it? Next, think about your chaser thoughts and find a way to weave your empowering statements into your new story. For every negative chaser thought, write the complete opposite into your story.

Before you rewrite your story, stop and ask for guidance. What is your heart telling you?

E.g. where you may have written 'I wish' or 'I want,' change your words to 'I have' or 'I enjoy.' Remember you can say what you want, so long as it is uplifting – you have the magic wand!

3 Action Steps

What can you do right NOW to make something in your magical life become real?

Work out three action steps and put them into your calendar to help you achieve your goals. Set reminders to stay focused.

....
....
....
....

....
....
....
....

....
....
....
....

My commitment to myself is:

I will complete each of these steps by .... (insert date)

I wear RED to remind myself of my action steps

THOUGHTS

Write or draw your thoughts

My Reward

How will you reward yourself once you have completed all three steps?

Make your reward something that you would not normally do for yourself so that when you have completed your three steps, you feel excited and enjoy your reward. Then use your excitement to create another three steps and keep your momentum going.

What happens if you don't complete your steps? (How will you feel?)

....
....
....

Congratulations!

How do you feel now that you are more aware of what lies in your heart? Do you feel happier within yourself than when you started your journal? Remember life is a journey. You are not rushing to be somewhere, you are on a journey to do, be and have, the best life you can experience. This is your purpose for your whole life, to enjoy as many moments as you can. To feel love and to give love. To be the best version of yourself that you can be. The more you love, especially yourself, the more life gives you to love. Happiness comes from within. It is not outside of you, it is not something you can purchase and no one has the power to make you happy, expect you. Choose to be happy, choose to live from love.

Take time to reflect through everything you have written. The more effort you put into this journal, the more you will get out of it. You can redo any of the pages every few months, especially if you are working on improving your clarity and awareness of thoughts. The journal gives you a reference point from where you started and then you can see how quickly your awareness grows and how your thoughts change.

You really can have a magical life, it's not hard, it just takes effort and commitment on your behalf. The great thing is you can think about most of these things wherever you are. If you are standing in a queue, stuck in traffic or simply washing your hair; you can think about raising your energy vibration, by thinking about what you love. You can choose to daydream about your wonderful life instead of replaying past hurts over and over. When your think good things, you hold a high energy vibration and you will inspire others to do the same.

It really is all up to you

The key to a great life is to be aware of your thoughts and feelings then align your true ones to your heart's desires

What's Next?

The RED Vision is the first part of a series of seven steps in following your heart to your pot of GOLD. The next step is ORANGE – My Experiences.

**How to create awesome experiences
Without stressing about time or money**

Orange is the way to enjoy your life to its fullest
even if you are busy or broke!

If you want to know more about ORANGE, then visit

www.sharondawn.com.au/orange

Either way, keep journaling.
Continue practicing every day to draw like a child
and write from within 💝

It really is the easiest way to learn how to follow your heart

Journal Time – Keep up the Magic

DRAW LIKE A CHILD

WRITE FROM WITHIN

DRAW LIKE A CHILD

WRITE FROM WITHIN

DRAW LIKE A CHILD

WRITE FROM WITHIN

DRAW LIKE A CHILD

WRITE FROM WITHIN

DRAW LIKE A CHILD

WRITE FROM WITHIN

DRAW LIKE A CHILD

WRITE FROM WITHIN

DRAW LIKE A CHILD

WRITE FROM WITHIN

DRAW LIKE A CHILD

WRITE FROM WITHIN

DRAW LIKE A CHILD

WRITE FROM WITHIN

DRAW LIKE A CHILD

WRITE FROM WITHIN

DRAW LIKE A CHILD

WRITE FROM WITHIN

DRAW LIKE A CHILD

WRITE FROM WITHIN

DRAW LIKE A CHILD

WRITE FROM WITHIN

DRAW LIKE A CHILD

WRITE FROM WITHIN

DRAW LIKE A CHILD

WRITE FROM WITHIN

DRAW LIKE A CHILD

WRITE FROM WITHIN

DRAW LIKE A CHILD

WRITE FROM WITHIN

DRAW LIKE A CHILD

WRITE FROM WITHIN

DRAW LIKE A CHILD

WRITE FROM WITHIN

DRAW LIKE A CHILD

WRITE FROM WITHIN

DRAW LIKE A CHILD

WRITE FROM WITHIN

DRAW LIKE A CHILD

WRITE FROM WITHIN

DRAW LIKE A CHILD

WRITE FROM WITHIN

DRAW LIKE A CHILD

WRITE FROM WITHIN

DRAW LIKE A CHILD

WRITE FROM WITHIN

When you think from love, you become love

Congratulations
on reaching the end of your journal

Well done! Now that you have completed all this in-depth work, don't let it slip away. Set up a daily ritual with the intention of topping up your energy vibration as a constant reminder of all the love and support you have no matter what is transpiring in your life.

Remember, you have the power to choose your thoughts and your responses; and with each, your energy vibration goes out to the universe and then reflects back to you. When you choose to think and respond from love, you get love. When you choose from fear, you get fear.

Being aware of your thoughts and feelings then choosing to align them with your true heart's desire, is what creates an awesome life. You have the power to do it, you just need to believe in yourself and practice it every day. When you choose to make it a way of life that you cherish, it will become your life, and that is when the magic really happens.

Don't forget your free gifts on page ix

To receive further support on your journey into awareness, go to
www.sharondawn.com.au

The ORANGE journal is next in this series and is about the fun experiences you want to have in your life. It is like working on your bucket list plus all your other dreams all put together. The journal builds on the things you love from RED and helps you work out what is most important and how you can bring those things into your life.

It is daydreaming with your inner child and it is loads of fun

Follow your heart and find your bliss.

NAMASTE
(I bow to the divine in you)

www.ingramcontent.com/pod-product-compliance
Lightning Source LLC
Chambersburg PA
CBHW061133010526
44107CB00068B/2921